Habitat Quality and Recruitment Success of Cui-ui in the Truckee River Downstream of Marble Bluff Dam, Pyramid Lake, Nevada

By G. Gary Scoppettone, Peter H. Rissler, J. Antonio Salgado, and Beverly Harry

Open-File Report 2013–1247

U.S. Department of the Interior
U.S. Geological Survey

U.S. Department of the Interior
SALLY JEWELL, Secretary

U.S. Geological Survey
Suzette M. Kimball, Acting Director

U.S. Geological Survey, Reston, Virginia: 2013

For more information on the USGS—the Federal source for science about the Earth,
its natural and living resources, natural hazards, and the environment—visit
http://www.usgs.gov or call 1–888–ASK–USGS

For an overview of USGS information products, including maps, imagery, and publications,
visit http://www.usgs.gov/pubprod

To order this and other USGS information products, visit http://store.usgs.gov

Suggested citation:
Scoppettone, G.G., Rissler, P.H., Salgado, J.S., and Harry, Beverly, 2013, Habitat quality and
recruitment success of cui-ui in the Truckee River downstream of Marble Bluff Dam, Pyramid Lake,
Nevada: U.S. Geological Survey Open-File Report 2013-1247, 22 p. ,
http://pubs.usgs.gov/of/2013/1247/.

Contents

Figures

Conversion Factors and Datum

Multiply	By	To obtain
Length		
centimeter (cm)	0.3937	inch (in.)
millimeter (mm)	0.03937	inch (in.)
meter (m)	3.281	foot (ft)
kilometer (km)	0.6214	mile (mi)
Area		
square kilometer (km^2)	0.3861	acre
Volume		
cubic meter (m^3)	35.31	cubic foot (ft^3)
liter (L)	1.057	quarts

Datum

Horizontal coordinate information is referenced to the insert datum name (and abbreviation) here for instance, "North American Datum of 1983 (NAD 83)."

Habitat Quality and Recruitment Success of Cui-ui in the Truckee River Downstream of Marble Bluff Dam, Pyramid Lake, Nevada

By G. Gary Scoppettone[1], Peter H. Rissler[1], and J. Antonio Salgado[1], and Beverly Harry[2]

Abstract

We compared cui-ui (*Chasmistes cujus*) recruitment from two reaches of the Truckee River with histories of severe erosional downcutting caused by a decline in Pyramid Lake surface elevation. In 1975, Marble Bluff Dam (MBD) was constructed 5 kilometers upstream of the extant mouth of the Truckee River to stabilize the upstream reach of the river; the downstream reach of the river remained unstable and consequently unsuitable for cui-ui recruitment. By the early 2000s, there was a decrease in the Truckee River's slope from MBD to Pyramid Lake after a series of wet years in the 1990s. This was followed by changes in river morphology and erosion abatement. These changes led to the question as to cui-ui recruitment potential in the Truckee River downstream of MBD. In 2012, more than 7,000 cui-ui spawners were passed upstream of MBD, although an indeterminate number of cui-ui spawned downstream of MBD. In this study, we compared cui-ui recruitment upstream and downstream of MBD during a Truckee River low-flow year (2012). Cui-ui larvae emigration to Pyramid Lake began earlier and ended later downstream of MBD. A greater number of cui-ui larvae was produced downstream of MBD than upstream. This also was true for native Tahoe sucker (*Catostomus tahoensis*) and Lahontan redside (*Richardsonius egregius*). The improved Truckee River stability downstream of MBD and concomitant cui-ui recruitment success is attributed to a rise in Pyramid Lake's surface elevation. A decline in lake elevation may lead to a shift in stream morphology and substrate composition to the detriment of cui-ui reproductive success as well as the reproductive success of other native fishes.

---

[1] U.S. Geological Survey.
[2] Environmental Department, Pyramid Lake Paiute Tribe of the Pyramid Lake Reservation, Nevada.

Introduction

Cui-ui (*Chasmistes cujus*) is a federally listed endangered species endemic to Pyramid Lake, Nevada, and it is culturally important to the Pyramid Lake Paiute Tribe of the Pyramid Lake Reservation, Nevada, known as "Kooyooe tukadu" (Cui-ui eaters). The historical cui-ui population decline is attributed to failed reproduction indirectly caused by water diversion from the Truckee River, Pyramid Lake's only perennial tributary and spawning habitat for this lake-dwelling species (La Rivers, 1962; Koch, 1972; Scoppetttone and others, 1986). During most of the 20th century, an average of 50 percent of the Truckee River flow had been diverted from the river causing the lower Truckee River to become erosive as it entrenched to equilibrate to a subsiding Pyramid Lake (Born and Ritter, 1970; Glancy and others, 1972). Decline of Pyramid Lake surface elevation and concomitant deposition of massive amounts of eroded material at the mouth of the Truckee River caused the formation of an expansive shallow delta. In many years, spawning habitat was inaccessible to cui-ui due to low streamflow and shallow delta conditions; even in years when streamflow was sufficiently high for cui-ui to traverse the delta, there typically was reproductive failure due to an erosive stream bottom causing eggs to drift downstream and not mature (Scoppettone and others, 1986).

Situated approximately 5 km upstream of the mouth of the Truckee River, the Marble Bluff Dam (MBD) was completed in 1975 and has served to stabilize the extremely erosive river channel upstream of the dam (Scoppettone and Vinyard, 1991). The river from MBD to Pyramid Lake remained unstable, as evidenced by a shallow braided channel with eroded banks and virtually no riparian corridor. Nearly three decades since the construction of MBD, the river downstream of the dam has now exhibited signs of reaching some semblance of stability; it became far less erosive, less braided, and it narrowed, and a dense stand of non-native Saltcedar (*Tamarix ramosissima*) established along its banks. The apparent riverine stability suggested that the downstream reach might be suitable for cui-ui spawning, and a comparison of cui-ui recruitment upstream and downstream of MBD would be instructive. A secondary question was what effect the apparent downstream change had on the recruitment success of other Pyramid Lake/Truckee River native fishes, particularly the Lahontan redside (*Richardsonius egregius*), which appeared to be all but extirpated from Pyramid Lake (Vigg, 1981). In this study, we investigated the use of the Truckee River downstream of MBD for fish reproduction, emphasizing cui-ui. Because of its long history of severe erosion, hereafter referred to as instability, this reach of stream has been overlooked as a substantial contributor to cui-ui recruitment as well as that of other Pyramid Lake/Truckee River native fishes.

Study Area and Background

Pyramid Lake is approximately 487 km^2 and lies within the boundary of the Pyramid Lake Reservation in west-central Nevada, at the western edge of the Lahontan Basin. It is a terminal lake with water being lost through evaporation, and consequently its water is saline and alkaline (Galat and others, 1981). Pyramid Lake's only perennial tributary is the Truckee River, which flows from Lake Tahoe northeast 192 km to Pyramid Lake (fig. 1). Its primary water source is snowmelt and rainfall originating from the eastern side of the Sierra Nevada.

The Truckee River has the distinction of being the site of this Nation's first Bureau of Reclamation project, the Newlands Project (La Rivers, 1962; U.S. Fish and Wildlife Service, 1992). Completed in 1905, the project core was a transbasin diversion canal conveying Truckee River water to the Carson River Basin for eventual agricultural use in the Lahontan Valley, Nevada (La Rivers, 1962; U.S. Fish and Wildlife Service, 1992). Water is diverted into the Truckee Canal at Derby Dam about 60 km upstream of Pyramid Lake. Timely water releases to the Truckee Canal and numerous small diversions along the Truckee River are met by storage and release of water from a network of reservoirs, three of which are natural lakes (Lake Tahoe, Donner Lake, and Independence Lake) modified for water storage and release. Water stored in Stampede Reservoir primarily is dedicated to the Pyramid Lake fishery (Buchanan and Strekal, 1988; U.S. Fish and Wildlife Service, 1992).

Until the mid-1940s, the Truckee River fed two lakes: Winnemucca Lake received overflow from Pyramid Lake, but because of water diversion Winnemucca Lake dried by the 1940s (La Rivers, 1962), and Pyramid Lake's surface elevation declined as much as 26 m. A consequence of the surface elevation decline of Pyramid Lake was that the lower Truckee River became extremely erosive from its mouth upstream 16.5 km to Numana Dam (Glancy and others, 1972). This resulted in the loss of agricultural land on the Pyramid Lake Reservation; more than 90 percent of the sediment load transported to Pyramid Lake and the Truckee River delta originated downstream of Numana Dam (Glancy and others, 1972). The construction of MBD eventually abated the rampant erosion from river km 5 upstream to Numana Dam leaving only the downstream reach extremely erosive. However, the slope from the base of MBD to the surface of Pyramid Lake has decreased from 0.235 percent in spring 1975 to 0.074 percent in spring 2013, due to channel degradation (fig. A1) and a general increase in lake-surface elevation since 1975 (fig. A2). From spring 1975 to spring 2013, the stream channel elevation declined 8.6 m and Pyramid Lake's elevation rose more than 2 m. These changes in streambed and lake elevations led to some semblance of riverine stability as evidenced by elimination of braids, narrowing of the stream channel (fig. A3), and establishment of a riparian corridor albeit primarily comprised of Saltcedar.

Besides serving as a hydraulic control stabilizing the river upstream to Numana Dam, MBD serves to divert water down a 5 km long bypass [Marble Bluff Fishway (MBF)] to the shallow Truckee River delta (fig. 1). If fish successfully traverse the Truckee River delta, MBD has a fish lock system to move cui-ui upstream. When the delta is virtually impassable to migratory fish, the MBF is available. The MBF operates with flows of about 1.1 m^3/s, and it has "Ice Harbor" type ladders along its course. Generally, the MBF has been used by migrating cui-ui when Pyramid Lake elevation is less than 1,160 m. However, the MBF generally is open to cui-ui only in high water years (Scoppettone and others, 1986). With lake elevations greater than 1,160 m, cui-ui have successfully traversed the Truckee River delta; however, high-flow years typically elicit the greatest cui-ui migratory response (Scoppettone and others, 1986). Every year cui-ui migrate to the mouth of the Truckee River forming a prespawning aggregation, but in low-flow years, few cui-ui attempt a spawning migration up the river or MBF, and the aggregation eventually disperses and females undergo gametic atresia (Scoppettone and others, 2000).

Tahoe sucker (*Catostomus tahoensis*) is the only other species known to enter the Truckee River from Pyramid Lake in numbers substantial enough to spawn. Historically, there was a sizeable Lahontan cutthroat trout (*Oncorhynchus clarkii henshawi*) migration into the Truckee River, but the population was extirpated by the first half of the 20th century as a result of water diversion (Sumner, 1939). The Lahontan cutthroat trout fishery is currently sustained through hatchery stocking, and the number of trout migrating into the river to attempt to reproduce is relatively small. Pyramid Lake's high alkalinity has inhibited nonnative salmonids from establishing in the lake (Wright and others, 1993), and using the river to reproduce.

Materials and Methods

In 2012, more than 7,000 cui-ui spawners passed upstream of MBD, although an indeterminate number of cui-ui spawned downstream of MBD; MBF was operated in 2012 but was not used by cui-ui; a small number of Tahoe suckers passed over MBD (94 fish) and even less used the MBF (43 fish) (Tim Loux, U.S. Fish and Wildlife Service, written commun.). To evaluate the contribution to cui-ui larvae recruitment from the Truckee River reach downstream of MBD, we compared the contribution with recruitment upstream of the dam. For this comparison, we plankton netted cui-ui larvae 30 m downstream of MBD (MBD station) and near the Truckee River delta (Delta station; fig. 2). The downstream site was selected because it was the lowest river point in which nets could be placed within a well-defined channel with sufficient velocity to fish effectively. Nets were 2.4-m-long with a 50-cm-diameter mouth. They each had a removable PVC cylinder (larvae receptacle) 20 cm deep and 8.5 cm wide at the receiving end. The net mesh was 800 μm, and the PVC cylinder had 500-μm-mesh fiberglass along its length. Nets were fitted with a General Oceanic Digital Flow Meter and harness. At the MBD station, two nets were fished off a cable using a pulley system to deploy and retrieve the nets from fishing sites. One net was fished near the center of the river channel, 15–20 m from the north bank, and the other was 3–10 m from the north bank. There were 60 exposed baffles equally spaced horizontally and vertically projecting from the face of MBD, which randomly mixed larvae such that each net captured representative samples of larvae passing over the dam (Scoppettone and Rissler, 2012). At the Delta station, three nets were fished, each attached to metal t-bar fence posts that were spaced equidistantly across the channel.

We began plankton netting on May 3, 2012, at the Delta station and May 7, 2012, at the MBD station. Nets were fished Monday, Wednesday, and Friday for 5–10 minutes at hourly intervals from 2100 to 0100 each night. The counter number on the digital flow meter was recorded prior to net setting. Immediately after nets were pulled, contents from each of the larvae receptacles were placed in separate 18.9 L plastic buckets, and the ending count of the digital flow meter was recorded. Captured catostomid larvae were enumerated, and up to 50 randomly selected larvae were placed in a vial of 10 percent formalin for later species identification. Each vial contained a tag with date and time of capture along with the identifying number of the net.

Preserved catostomids were identified to species using a binocular dissecting scope and a key for catostomid larvae of the Truckee River Basin (Snyder, 1983). Number of larvae was counted for each net and each sample hour. Ten cui-ui were selected randomly from each vial and measured to the nearest 0.01 mm (total length). We also captured Lahontan redside larvae and juveniles in our nets; these were enumerated and released downstream of our nets. Enumerated catostomid larvae in excess of 50 also were released downstream of our nets.

We estimated number of cui-ui larvae emigrating past the MBD and Delta stations for the 2012 spawning year by first using the General Oceanic Digital Flow Meter to calculate the volume of water passed through each net for a 5–10 minute fishing period and then counting the catostomid larvae in each net sample. In the laboratory, we calculated the relative proportion of cui-ui to Tahoe sucker for each net set, and the number of cui-ui larvae captured was extrapolated to 1 hour. We then estimated number of cui-ui larvae/m^3 reaching the MBD and Delta stations during a 24-h period for each Monday, Wednesday, and Friday of sampling. We used a linear regression equation with the number of cui-ui larvae/m^3 captured over 24 h diel generated by Scoppettone and Rissler (2012) as the dependent variable, and the number of cui-ui larvae/m^3 in a 4-h sampling event as the independent variable. The estimated number of cui-ui larvae that passed the nets at the MBD and Delta stations on a given day was the product of the number of larvae/m^3 and total m^3 flowing past the two stations that day. The online National Water Information System of the U.S. Geological Survey (*http://waterdata.usgs.gov/nwis*) was used to track daily flow at the Nixon gaging station, 2 km upstream of MBD.

We extrapolated the daily larvae numbers to calculate larvae number for the season (estimated number of larvae for sampling days × number of days during migration/number of sampling days), following Scoppettone and Rissler (2012). To estimate the relative contribution of cui-ui larvae upstream of MBD to that downstream of the dam, we subtracted the estimated larvae capture at MBD from the estimated capture at the Delta station.

Too few Lahontan redside larvae were captured in our diel sampling to establish timing of their emigration so we used capture per unit effort to compare contributions to Lahontan redside larvae recruitment upstream and downstream of MBD. Catch per unit effort was the number of larvae captured/m^3 of water flowing through our plankton nets.

Substrate Downstream of Marble Bluff Dam

We quantified substrate composition at five transects (equally spaced 1,200 m apart) starting 300 to 5,100 m downstream of MBD, just upstream of the Delta station. In addition, each transect had five sites equally spaced between the streambanks along the Truckee River channel downstream of MBD, the river width at the five transects ranged from 26.5 to 50.0 m (fig. 2).This sampling scheme was selected to compare substrate changes along the course of the river. Samples were taken using a McNeil sampler (McNeil and Ahnell, 1964). From February 22 to March 5, 2013, a total of 25 core samples were collected and each sample was placed in a 7.6 L plastic bucket, spread out on plywood and allowed to air dry. Samples were then run through a series of 9 U.S.A. standard sieves with openings in the range of 50.3–0.83 mm.

Relative use classifications have not been established for cui-ui but they have for salmonids (McNeil and Ahnell, 1964), and we adapted this classification as a conservative means of assessing substrate suitability for cui-ui. The particle diameter breakdown is as follows: (1) cobble > 50.8 mm, (2) spawning gravel 50.8–6.3 mm, (3) fine gravel 6.3–0.83 mm, and (4) fines <0.83 mm.

Results

Larvae Recruitment Upstream and Downstream of Marble Bluff Dam

In 2012 (a dry hydrologic year), more cui-ui larvae were recruited from downstream of MBD (3.38×10^7) than upstream of the dam (2.76×10^7) (fig. 3). Capture success among nets varied substantially resulting in a standard deviation (SD) of 1.1×10^7 at the MBD station and 2.9×10^7 at the Delta station. Similarly, for Tahoe sucker, a greater number of emigrating larvae arrived at the Delta station (2.5×10^6, SD = 2.6×10^6) than at the MBD station (1.5×10^6, SD = 6.6×10^5), and catch per unit effort of Lahontan redside larvae was greater at the Delta station (0.055 larvae/m^3) than at the MBD station (0.003 larvae/m^3).

Emigration Patterns

Cui-ui emigration began earlier and ended later downstream of MBD. The first cui-ui larvae were netted May 3, 2012, and the last on July 16, 2012, at the Delta station; the first cui-ui larvae were netted on May 14, 2012, and the last on June 11, 2012 at the MBD station (fig. A4). Likewise, duration of emigration was slightly longer at the Delta station for Tahoe sucker and Lahontan redside compared to the MBD station (figs. A5, A6). Peak emigration for cui-ui was May 21, 2012, at both stations. Peak emigration for Tahoe sucker was June 17, 2012, at the MBD station and June 21, 2012, at the Delta station. Lahontan redside were captured in greatest abundance on May 24, 2012, the first day they were captured at the Delta station.

Substrate Composition

Our substrate samples give a cross sectional profile of substrate composition at five equally spaced transects along the Truckee River downstream of MBD. Analysis for each of the five sites at each of five transects is given in the appendix (table A1). Average percentage of spawning gravel for the five sample transects ranged from 16 to 60 percent. There was a general tendency for spawning gravel to increase in an upstream direction and fines to decrease but the difference was not significant (df = 4, t = 2.31, p = 0.08) (fig. 4). Some gravel bars were rich in spawning gravels with estimates as high as 77 percent immediately downstream of MBD. Gravel bars tended to occur at the upstream three sampling transects, and in March 2013, we observed spawning Lahontan cutthroat trout and their redds at three different gravel bars within 1,500 m of MBD (fig. 2).

Discussion

This study contributes to assessing the suitability of the Truckee River downstream of MBD for recruitment of cui-ui and other native fish species. In the low water year of 2012, we calculated that 10 percent more cui-ui larvae were produced downstream of MBD than upstream. Furthermore, we speculate that larvae downstream of MBD had a higher survival rate than those produced upstream for the following reasons. First the potential injury, trauma, or death from dropping over the height of MBD (approximately 7 m in 2012) and baffles was avoided (Scoppettone and others, 1986). Secondly, emigrating larvae recruited downstream of MBD would likely enter Pyramid Lake with greater weight and associated greater energy reserves by traveling a shorter distance to the lake. Cui-ui larvae mouths open approximately a day or two after swim-up (Koch, 1972; Koch and Contreras, 1973; Bres, 1978), and those cui-ui larvae close to the lake would be positioned in littoral habitat to feed by the time they had the ability to feed. Houde (2002) found that among fishes even modest larvae size advantage translates into greater fitness advantage.

More than 90 percent of the emigrating fish larvae captured in our plankton nets at the MBD and Delta stations were cui-ui. Cui-ui's disproportionally large number of emigrating larvae is attributed to its life history characteristics. Cui-ui are larger, longer lived and more fecund than Tahoe sucker and Lahontan redside (Scoppettone, 1988; Moyle, 2002), allowing it to endure a greater number of years in Pyramid Lake without successful recruitment (Scoppettone and others, 1986), and females continue to grow and consequently become more fecund. Furthermore, adult cui-ui probably are sufficiently large that they are not prey to most Lahontan cutthroat trout inhabiting the lake and experience little mortality there. Lahontan redside are smaller, less fecund, and shorter lived than either cui-ui or Tahoe sucker (Scoppettone, 1988; Moyle, 2002) and numerically probably least represented in Pyramid Lake. Cui-ui are obligate lake dwellers; Tahoe sucker and Lahontan redside inhabit stream habitat as well, but we suspect that there are lake forms of these species, and the lake form decline is due to lack of access to spawning habitat.

This study suggests that when Pyramid Lake is sufficiently high to allow river access, the reach of the Truckee River downstream of MBD is a contributor to Pyramid Lake's Tahoe sucker and Lahontan redside recruitment. The river also is recruiting Tahoe sucker and Lahontan redside (as well as cui-ui) along a river reach in which virtually no fish larvae had been recruited in decades. If lake level does not decline such that the Truckee River remains fairly stable, this reach may contribute to the enhancement of populations of the lake form of Tahoe sucker and Lahontan redside in Pyramid Lake.

Knowledge of timing larvae emigration success for cui-ui in relation to Tahoe sucker and Lahontan Reside is important for managing water to promote the emigration success of all three species. In the low-flow year of 2012, Tahoe sucker larvae were sparsely represented, and their emigration occurred approximately 1 month after cui-ui. Lahontan redside larvae were so few in number, and most were captured in 1 day, that that we were unable to discern a distinctive emigration pattern. Timing of emigration of the three species should be monitored in the future when the populations of Tahoe sucker and Lahontan redside are more robust. The water management plan for the Pyramid Lake fishery would benefit from knowledge of the respective emigration patterns of cui-ui, Tahoe sucker, and Lahontan redside larvae into Pyramid Lake over a broader seasonal sampling period (that is, February through August) and under different flow regimes representing a range of wet to dry water years.

Recruitment of cui-ui larvae and other native fishes downstream of MBD observed in this study is a good indicator that this stream reach had arrived at some semblance of hydraulic stability. Another indicator is the composition of bottom substrate. There is no quantitative study pertaining to the changes in substrate composition downstream of MBD over time, but it is our qualitative assessment that bottom substrate has changed from a predominantly sandy bottom following the construction of MBD to a more gravel bottom in recent years. Samples taken at the five transects along the river indicated that gravel (6.3–50.0 mm diameter) predominated the sample reach. This is important because cui-ui spawn in flowing water over gravel substrate (Scoppettone and others, 1983; Scoppettone and others, 1986). This is much like the conditions favored by salmonids and, indeed, several pairs of Lahontan cutthroat trout were observed spawning in gravel downstream of MBD during this study (fig. 2).

The condition of the Truckee River downstream of MBD not only influences cui-ui reproduction potential, but probably adult cui-ui survival as well. Under unstable river conditions (wide, braided, and erosive channel lacking a riparian corridor), this river reach has been a site of substantial adult mortality from American White Pelican (*Pelecanus erythrorhynchos)* predation and occasional stranding (fig. A7). River stability downstream of MBD is primarily a function of stream gradient (Born and Ritter, 1970); greater slope translates into greater energy to move small-particle substrate (Morisawa, 1968).

The stream slope downstream of MBD likely changes on an annual basis as lake level changes. At the time of this study, trajectory of the slope was one of increase (associated with low annual discharge) and a declining lake level. The slope increase has not been sufficient to revert to a broad and braided channel with a transient stream bottom. However, continued lake level decline may cause a reversion to a stream reach with increased hazard to migrating fish and decrease in recruitment potential. A rise in lake level from the 1,159 m in this study would likely continue to enhance stream stability, until lake level reached about 1,163.4 m, inundating the stream reach (U.S. Department of Interior, 2011). Inundation would greatly reduce (if not preclude) cui-ui reproduction (Chatto, 1979), but greatly facilitate fish passage into the Truckee River for fish species migrating from Pyramid Lake. Lake elevation greater than 1,163.4 m also would greatly increase spawner survival by reducing American White Pelican predation, as pelicans are not diving birds and typically capture their prey in water depths of a meter or less (Evans and Knopf, 1993).

This study took place during a dry water year, and few cui-ui attempted a spawning migration; thus that portion of the study plan meant to determine what proportion of spawners spawn upstream of MBD compared to that spawning downstream could not be quantified. This information also is critical in estimating survival from egg deposition to emigrating fry produced. Judging from the quality of gravels downstream of MBD, the quality of substrate does not appear to be a variable to limit survival when contrasted to substrate upstream of MBD. We recommend conducting studies on cui-ui reproductive success downstream of MBD related to change in lake level and flow regime. This information would be helpful in managing streamflow into Pyramid Lake for the benefit of the cui-ui fishery as well as for other Pyramid Lake/Truckee River native fishes.

Acknowledgments

We thank the Pyramid Lake Paiute Tribe for giving us the privilege of working on their lake and river to study cui-ui. Thanks to Danielle Johnson, Mark Hereford, Mark Fabes, and Eric Miskow for assisting in the plankton netting. We thank Tom Strekal, Stefanie Scoppettone, and Mark Fabes for reviewing the manuscript.

References Cited

Born, S.M., and Ritter, D.F., 1970, Modern terrace development near Pyramid Lake, Nevada, and its geologic implications: Geological Society of America Bulletin, v. 81, p. 1,233–1,242.

Bres, M., 1978, The embryonic development of the cui-ui, *Chasmistes cujus* (Teleostei, Catostomidae): Reno, University of Nevada, M.S. thesis, 23 p.

Buchanan, C.C., and Strekal, T.A., 1988, Simulated water management and evaluation procedures for cui-ui (*Chasmistes cujus*): Reno and Carson City, Nev., U.S. Fish and Wildlife Service and Bureau of Reclamation, 47 p. and app.

Chatto, D.A., 1979, Effects of salinity on hatching success of the cui-ui: Progressive Fish-Culture, v. 41, p. 82–85.

Evans, R. M., and Knopf, F.L., 1993, American White Pelican: The Birds of North America v. 57, p. 1-20.

Galat, D.L., Lider, E.L., Vigg, S., and Roberston, S.R., 1981, Limnology of a large, deep North American terminal lake, Pyramid Lake, Nevada, U.S.A.: Hydrobiologia, v. 82, p. 281–317.

Glancy, P.A., Van Denburgh, A.S., and Born, S.M., 1972, Runoff, erosion, and solutes in the lower Truckee River, Nevada, during 1969: Water Resources Bulletin, v. 8, p. 1,157–1,172.

Houde, E.D., 2002, Mortality, *in* Fuiman, L.A. and Werner, R.G., eds., Fishery science—The unique contributions of early life stage: Malden, Mass., Blackwell Science Ltd., p. 64–87.

Koch, D.L., 1972, Life history information on the cui-ui lakesucker (*Chasmistes cujus* Cope, 1883) endemic to Pyramid Lake, Washoe County, Nevada: Reno, University of Nevada, 343 p.

Koch, D.L., and Contreras, G.P., 1973, Hatching technique for the cui-ui lakesucker (*Chasmistes cujus* Cope, 1883): Progressive Fish-Culture, v. 35, p. 61–63.

La Rivers, I., 1962, Fishes and fisheries of Nevada: Reno, Nevada Fish and Game Commission, Reno, 88 p.

McNeil, W.J., and Ahnell, W.H., 1964, Success of pink salmon spawning relative to size of spawning material: U.S. Fish and Wildlife Service Special Scientific Report, Fisheries, no. 469, 15 p.

Morisawa, M., 1968, Streams—Their dynamics and morphology: New York, McGraw-Hill, Earth and Planetary Science Series, 175 p.

Moyle, P.B., 2002, Inland fishes of California: Berkeley, University of California Press, 405 p.

Scoppettone, G.G., 1988, Growth and longevity of cui-ui (*Chasmistes cujus*) and longevity in other catostomids and cyprinids: Transactions of the American Fisheries Society v. 117, p. 301–307.

Scoppettone, G.G., Coleman M., and Wedemeyer, G.A., 1986, Life history and status of the endangered cui-ui of Pyramid Lake, Nevada: U.S. Fish and Wildlife Service, Fish and Wildlife Research 1, 23 p.

Scoppettone, G.G., Rissler, P.H., and Buettner, M.E., 2000, Reproductive longevity and fecundity associated with nonannual spawning in cui-ui: Transactions of the American Fisheries Society, v. 129, p. 658–669.

Scoppettone, G.G., Wedemeyer, G.A., Coleman, M., and Burge, H., 1983, Reproduction by the endangered cui-ui in the lower Truckee River: Transactions of the American Fisheries Society v.112, p. 788–793.

Scoppettone, G.G., and Rissler, P.H., 2012, Cui-ui reproductive success from potential egg deposition to larval emigration: Western North American Naturalist, v. 72, p. 286–295.

Scoppettone, G.G., and Vinyard, G., 1991, Life history and management of four endangered lacustrine suckers, *in* Minckley, W.L., and Deacon, J.E., eds., Battle against extinction— Native fish management in the American West: Tucson: University of Arizona Press, p. 359–377.

Snyder, D.E., 1983, Identification of catostomid larvae in Pyramid Lake and the Truckee River, Nevada: Transactions of the American Fisheries Society v.112, p. 333-348.

Sumner, F.H., 1939, The decline of the Pyramid Lake fishery: Transactions of the American Fisheries Society, v. 69, p. 216–224.

U.S. Department of Interior, 2011, COE feasibility level fish bypass design at Marble Bluff Dam, Bureau of Reclamation: Denver, Colo., Hydraulic Laboratory Report HL-2011-01, 38 p., plus app.

U.S. Fish and Wildlife Service, 1992, Cui-ui (*Chamistes cujus*) recovery plan, 2nd revision: Portland, Oregon, U.S. Fish and Wildlife Service, 47 p., plus app.

Vigg, 1981, Species composition and relative abundance of adult fish in Pyramid Lake, Nevada, Great Basin Nat. v.41, p. 395-408.

Wright, P., Iwama, G.K., and Wood, C.M., 1993, Ammonia and urea excretion in Lahontan cutthroat trout (*Oncorhynchus clarki henshawi*) adapted to the highly alkaline Pyramid Lake (pH 9.4): Journal of Experimental Biology, v. 175, p. 153–172.

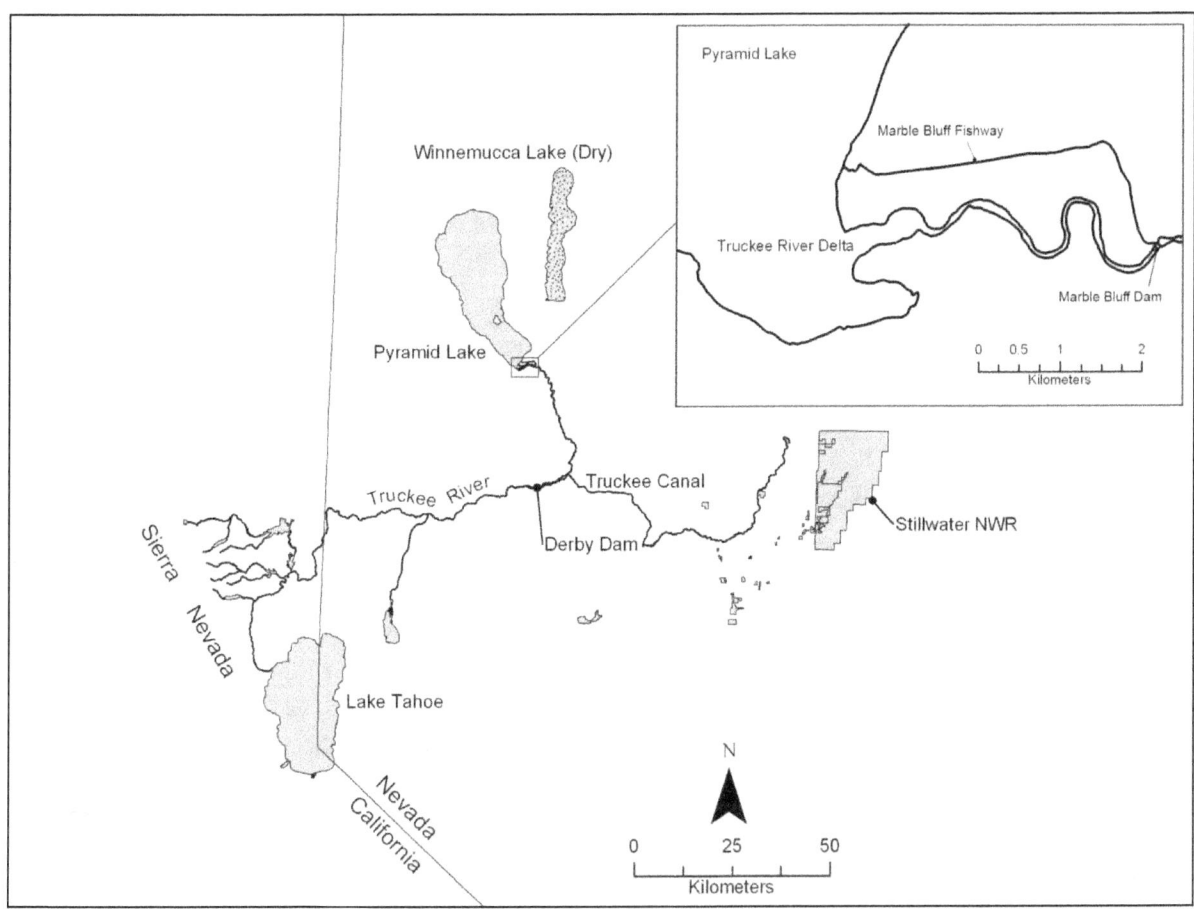

Figure 1. Study reach in relation to the Truckee River/Pyramid Lake system. Inset: Truckee River study reach in relation to Marble Bluff Dam and Marble Bluff Fishway.

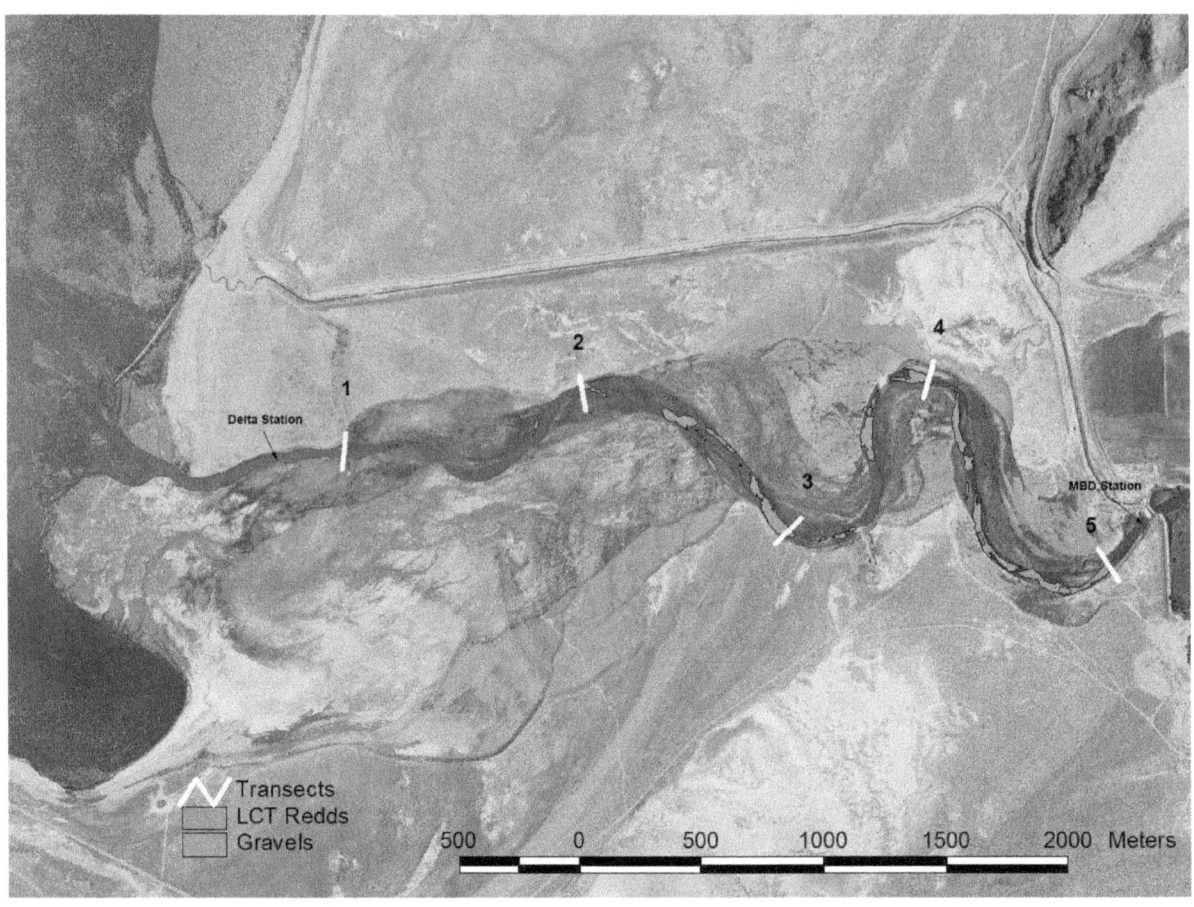

Figure 2. Aerial photograph (2010) of the Truckee River downstream of Marble Bluff Dam showing five sampling transects (yellow), gravel bars (blue), and Lahontan Cutthroat Trout (LCT) redds (red) with Delta and Marble Bluff Dam plankton sampling stations.

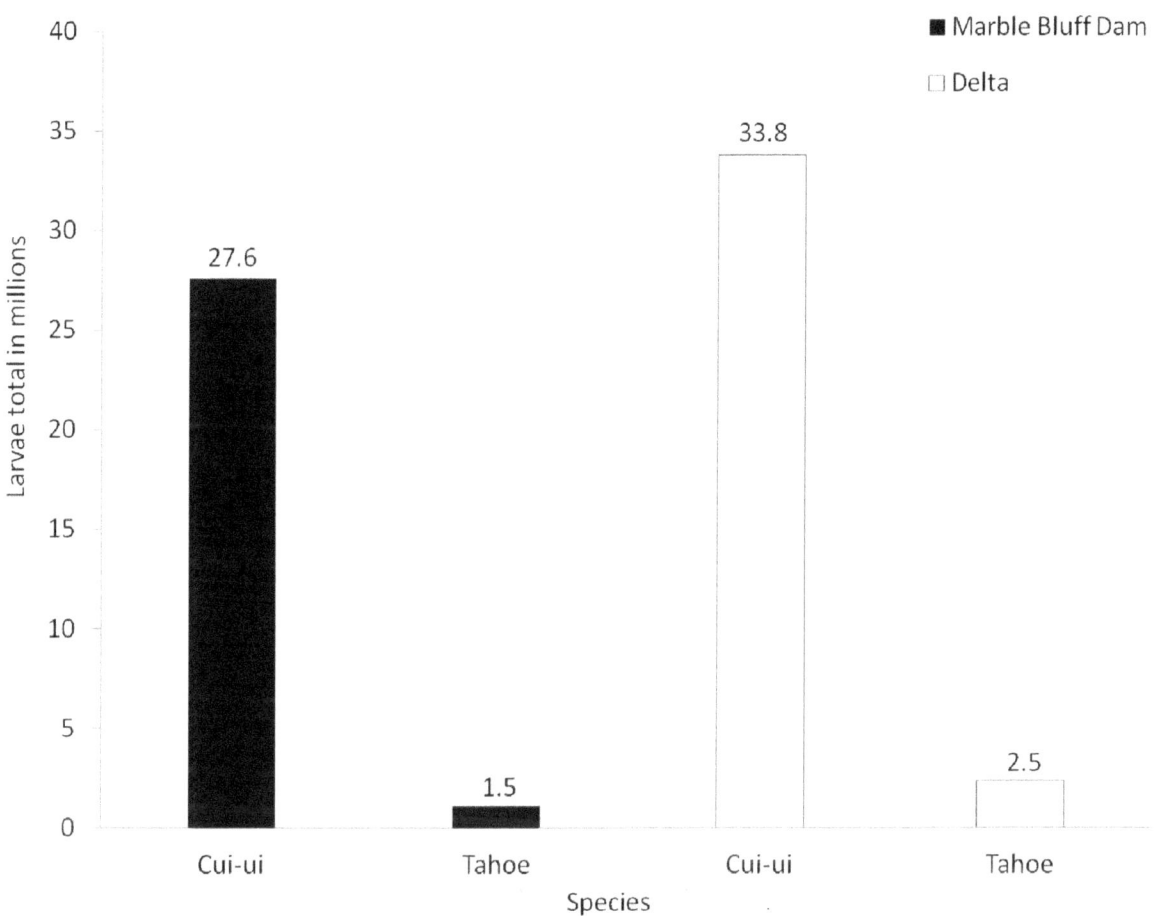

Figure 3. Number of cui-ui and Tahoe sucker larvae recruited from the Truckee River upstream and downstream of Marble Bluff Dam in 2012, as measured at the Marble Bluff Dam station and Delta station.

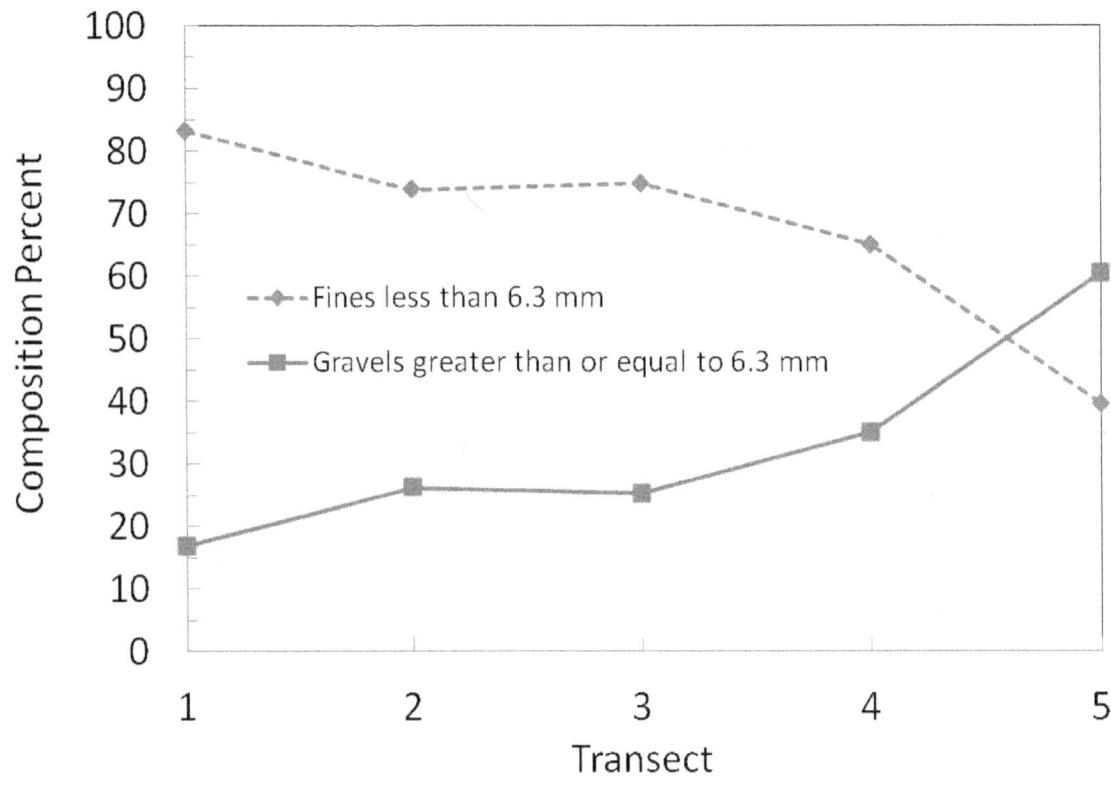

Figure 4. Relative percentage of fines and gravels at five sites along the Truckee River downstream of Marble Bluff Dam for samples taken from February 22 to March 5, 2013.

Appendix

Figure A1. Marble Bluff Dam during construction in 1976 – no energy dissipation baffles showing (top photograph, USFWS). Marble Bluff Dam in 2002 (bottom photograph, USGS). Stream degradation has caused exposure of energy dissipation baffles.

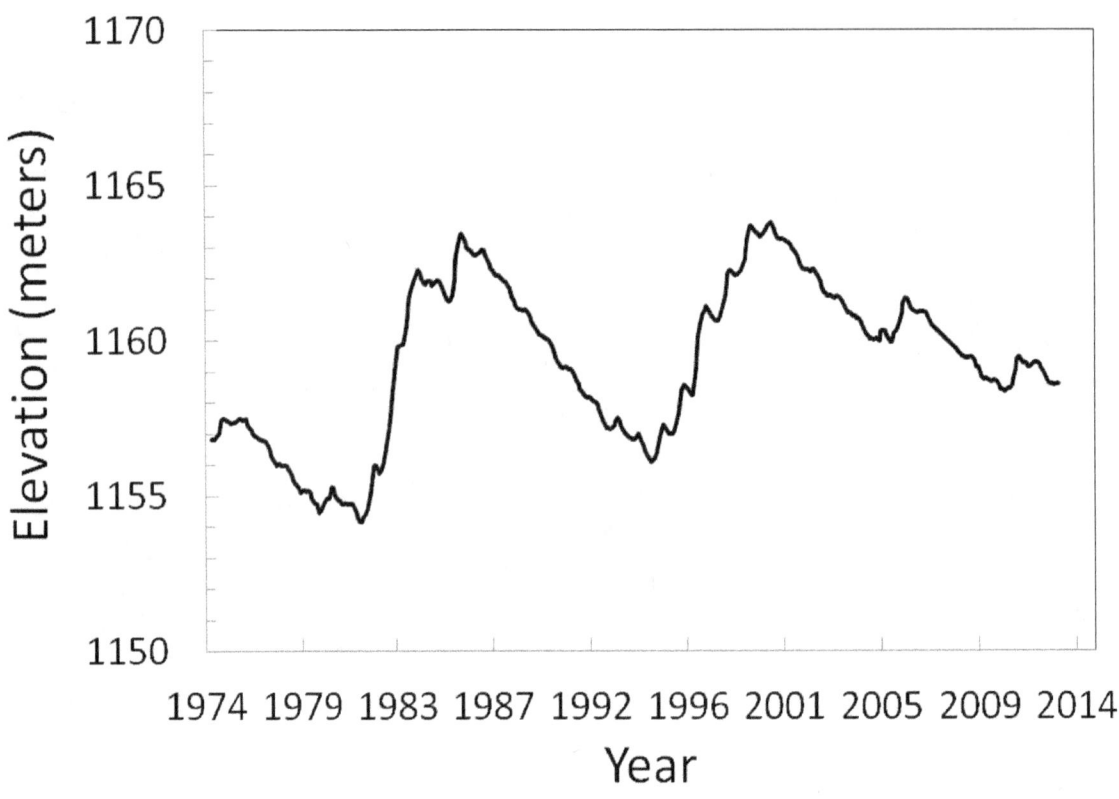

Figure A2. Pyramid Lake spring time surface elevations from 1975 (1,156.81 m) the year Marble Bluff Dam and Fishway were completed, to the present (1,158.59 m).

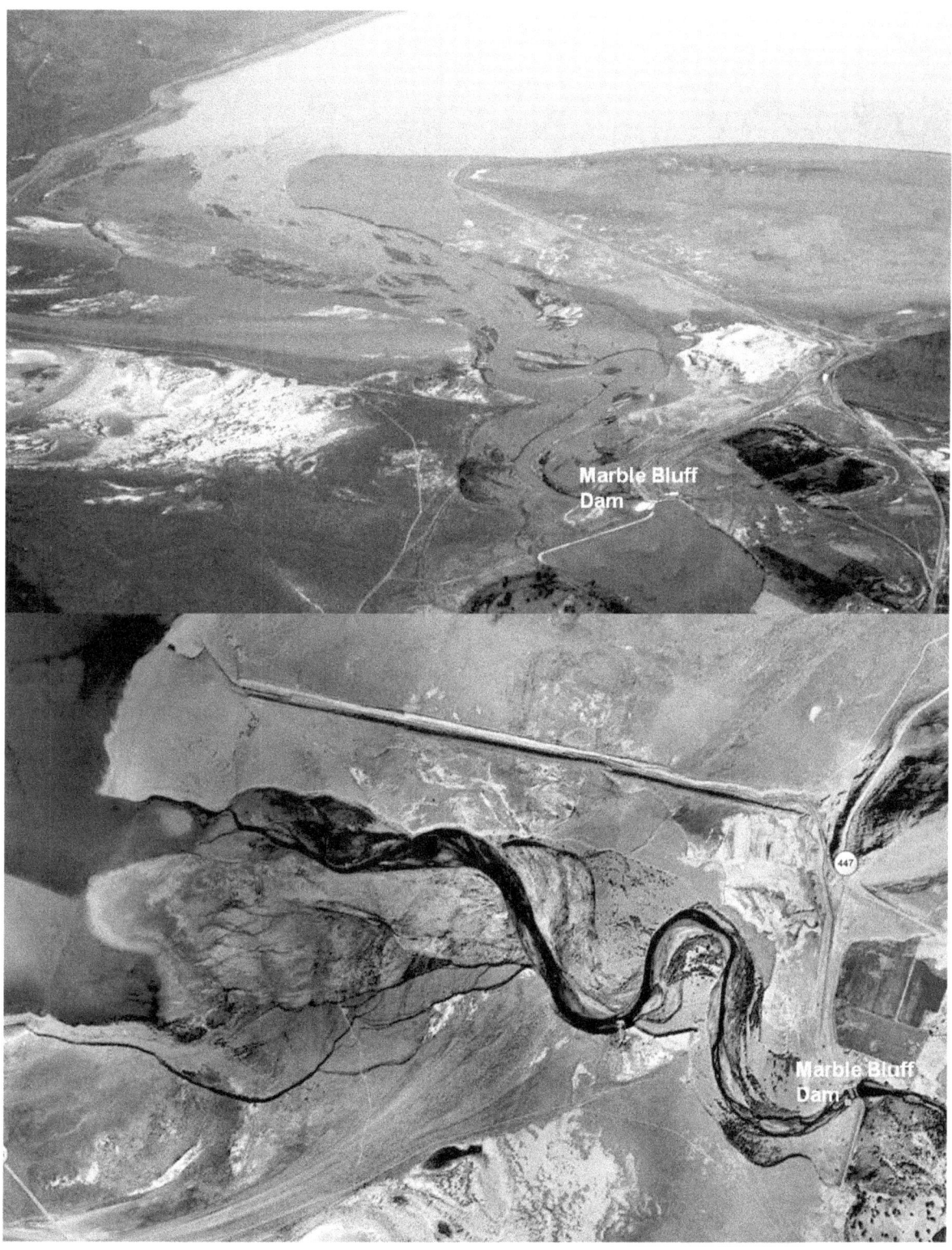

Figure A3. Truckee River downstream of Marble Bluff Dam in 1982, illustrating lack of bank stability (top photograph, USGS). Truckee River downstream of Marble Bluff Dam in 2006 illustrating bank stability (bottom photograph, taken from Google Earth).

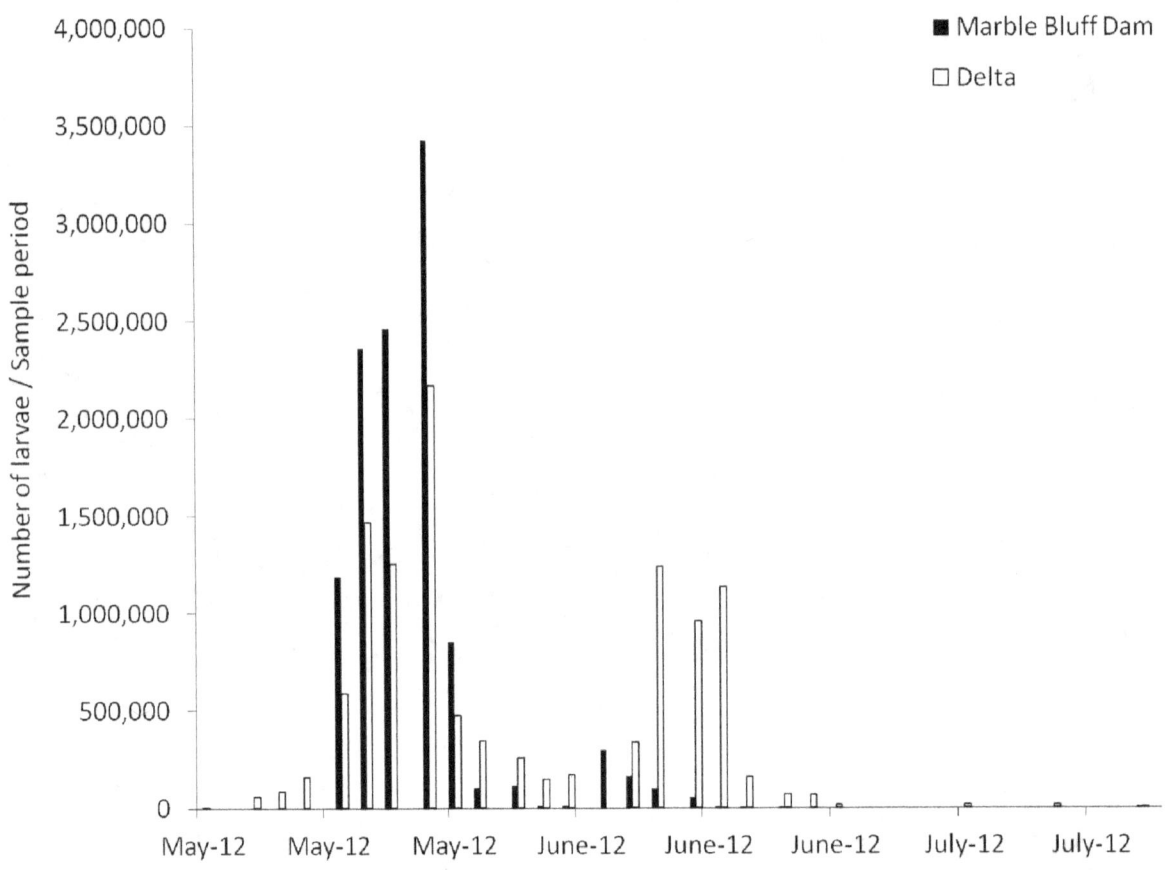

Figure A4. Emigration pattern of cui-ui larvae at Marble Bluff Dam and Delta stations.

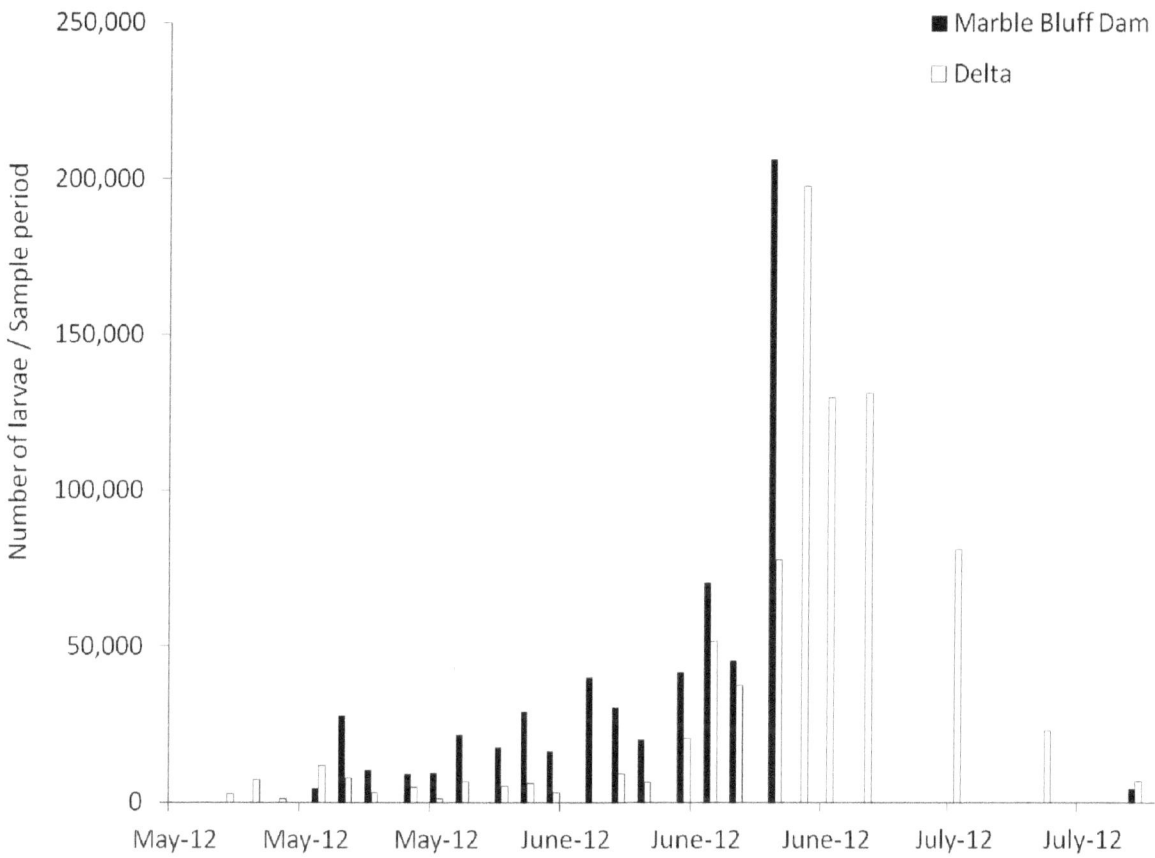

Figure A5. Emigration pattern of Tahoe sucker larvae at Marble Bluff Dam and Delta stations.

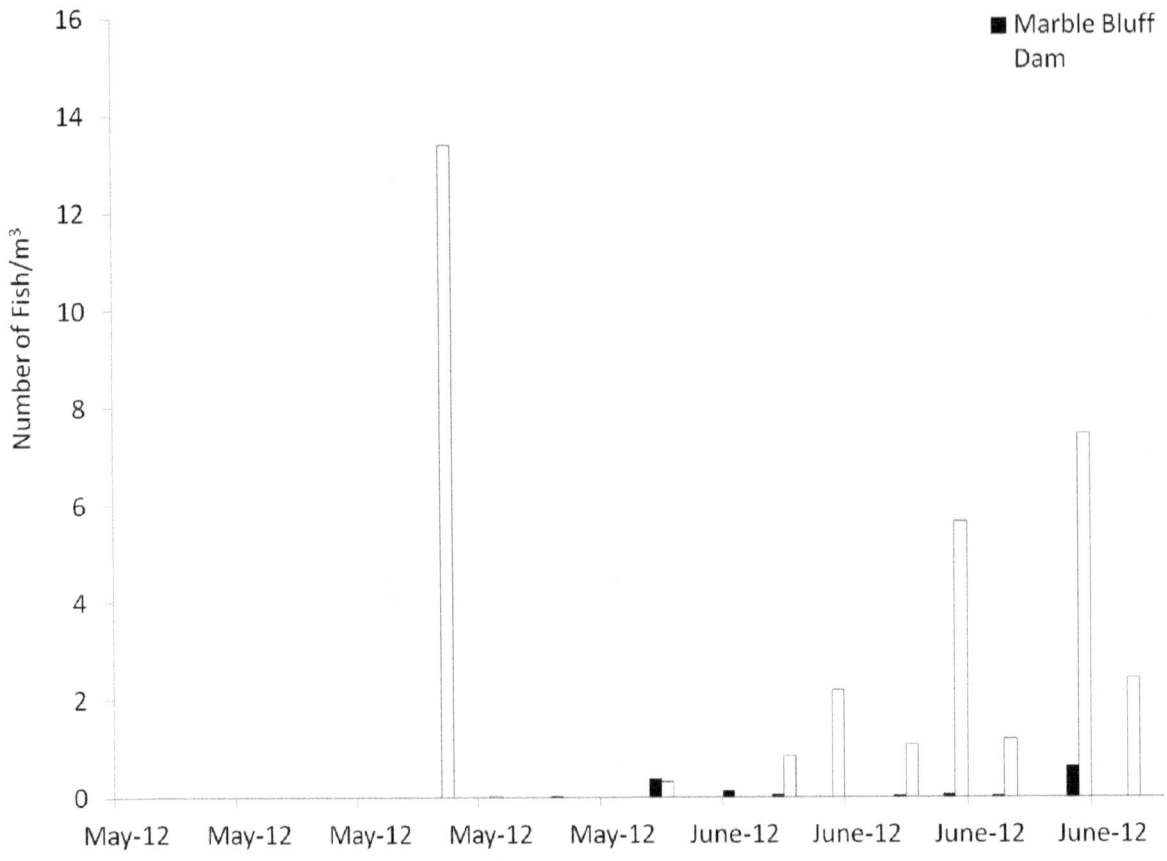

Figure A6. Emigration pattern of Lahontan redside larvae at Marble Bluff Dam and Delta stations.

Figure A7. American White Pelican preying on cui-ui near Truckee River delta (top photograph, Mike Sevon, MikeSevonPhotos.com). Cui-ui left stranded in braided shifting channel (bottom photograph, USGS).

Table A1. Substrate percent composition for five Truckee River transects with five stations each.

[Percentages may not sum to 100 due to rounding]

		Substrate diameter (millimeter)							
Transect	Station	<0.425	0.425	0.85	1.7	6.3	12.5	25	50
1	1	6.81	15.05	11.11	25.09	18.64	18.28	5.02	0.00
1	2	0.00	22.12	37.61	31.42	8.85	0.00	0.00	0.00
1	3	10.10	30.30	28.28	26.26	4.04	1.01	0.00	0.00
1	4	20.41	59.18	18.37	2.04	0.00	0.00	0.00	0.00
1	5	8.11	46.85	29.73	9.01	3.60	2.70	0.00	0.00
2	1	24.00	14.15	13.85	20.62	13.54	9.54	4.31	0.00
2	2	9.30	24.42	24.42	29.07	8.14	4.65	0.00	0.00
2	3	10.27	21.88	16.07	24.11	20.54	7.14	0.00	0.00
2	4	13.86	50.60	12.65	15.66	6.02	1.20	0.00	0.00
2	5	6.79	18.87	12.83	17.36	14.34	20.38	9.43	0.00
3	1	76.09	13.04	6.52	3.73	0.62	0.00	0.00	0.00
3	2	2.44	78.88	4.54	5.93	4.54	2.97	0.70	0.00
3	3	4.53	18.11	13.58	22.26	15.09	15.85	3.77	6.79
3	4	8.15	13.33	8.89	17.04	18.52	26.67	7.41	0.00
3	5	9.59	13.28	8.86	21.40	17.71	21.77	3.69	3.69
4	1	76.40	8.99	1.12	3.37	6.74	2.25	1.12	0.00
4	2	5.39	8.82	9.31	20.59	16.67	24.51	9.80	4.90
4	3	5.34	12.62	7.77	15.53	16.50	29.13	13.11	0.00
4	4	6.85	22.60	9.59	16.44	13.70	23.97	6.85	0.00
4	5	98.74	0.84	0.42	0.00	0.00	0.00	0.00	0.00
5	1	0.00	0.00	9.15	14.24	29.15	30.17	9.49	7.80
5	2	0.00	0.00	26.36	20.91	20.91	20.00	11.82	0.00
5	3	0.00	12.92	14.02	23.62	19.93	19.93	9.59	0.00
5	4	0.00	6.90	20.00	15.17	17.24	26.21	14.48	0.00
5	5	12.85	8.43	6.83	9.24	11.65	17.67	33.33	0.00